HISTORIC APARTMENT BUILDINGS
OF SALT LAKE CITY

Copyright © 2016 by Lisa Michele Church

All rights reserved. No part of this publication may be reproduced, distributed, or transmitted in any form or by any means, including photocopying, recording, or other electronic or mechanical methods, without the prior written permission of the author, except in the case of brief quotations embodied in critical reviews and certain other noncommercial uses permitted by copyright law.

Cover, Book Layout and Design by Kent Hepworth, kent@worthdesigninginc.com

Editing by Laurieann Thorpe

Photographs on pages 12 and 13 are property of the Utah State Historical Society and are used with their permission.

All other text and photographs by Lisa Michele Church www.relentlesshistory.com

Printed in the United States of America

Portions of this book were previously published in the Utah Historical Quarterly, Winter 2016 issue, Volume 84, Number 1, "Historic Salt Lake City Apartments of the Early Twentieth Century," by Lisa Michele Church, and as part of a brochure of the same name published by the Utah Division of State History in September, 2015.

HISTORIC APARTMENT BUILDINGS
OF SALT LAKE CITY

Text and Photography by
LISA MICHELE CHURCH

Layout and Design by
KENT HEPWORTH

CONTENTS

9 INTRODUCTION
"There's Always Somebody Home" – Early 20th Century Apartment Buildings of Salt Lake City

19 SECTION ONE
Bold Beginnings

51 SECTION TWO
Building Boom

67 SECTION THREE
Dramatic Designs

83 SECTION FOUR
Elegant to the End

102 MAP

104 MAP LIST

106 INDEX

108 SOURCES AND NOTES

109 BIBLIOGRAPHY

INTRODUCTION

The lovely streetscapes of downtown Salt Lake City feature historic apartment buildings on nearly every block. I began photographing them in 2006 as I was researching family stories. My parents lived in the Los Gables Apartments as newlyweds in the 1950s; I lived in the Council Crest Apartments as a college student in the 1970s. I walked around the buildings studying their stone work, quirky architecture and antique lighting. I fell in love with their style and determined to photograph every one. This volume is intended to document Salt Lake City's historic apartment buildings still standing within the grid from Main Street to Thirteenth East, and from Fourth South to Third Avenue. The building exteriors were my focus in this effort; perhaps another volume will cover the interiors. To me, the architectural beauty of a building itself creates a powerful image.

I realized that each building echoes with the sounds of the people who passed through it. Along with capturing photographs, I looked into some of the residents' stories. To find the fragments of lives within the apartment walls, I chose the names of random residents listed in the Polk's Salt Lake City directories during the period between 1920 and 1960. I researched those residents through the U.S. Census, the birth and death records, and the local newspapers. Each resident's story was fascinating in its own right, but as a story that occurred in an historic Salt Lake City apartment building, it told an even richer tale of personal memories entwined with enduring buildings.

–Lisa Michele Church, 2016

THERE'S ALWAYS SOMEBODY HOME
EARLY 20TH CENTURY APARTMENT BUILDINGS OF SALT LAKE CITY

BY LISA MICHELE CHURCH

Salt Lake City contains many beautiful examples of early 20th Century apartment buildings constructed to house a growing urban population between 1900 and 1940. With whimsical names such as the Piccadilly, the Peter Pan, and the Waldorf, these buildings beckoned to Utahns who were interested in a new approach to residential life. Apartments became places of beginnings and endings. Whether you were a young couple starting out your marriage, a single woman leaving home for the first time, or an immigrant finally finding work in America, an apartment was just the right mix of permanency and impermanency. It felt like a home, but not necessarily *your* home.

As one early resident put in, "You move in with a suitcase; you move out with a truck."[1] Salt Lake's early urban apartments were usually occupied by members of the city's middle class and offered people modern luxuries they may not have been able to afford previously.[2] The apartments featured innovative amenities such as Murphy "disappearing beds,"[3] Frigidaire refrigerators, electric ranges, and laundry facilities. The interiors were also upscale, some with French doors, elegant balconies, chandeliers and mosaic tile foyers.[4]

"The building will be steam heated, you will have hot water ready at all times of day or night, as well as free janitor and night watchman service, telephone and gas range…you will save on coal bills, water, telephone, street car fares and other incidentals, will reduce your cost of living, and you will have all the comforts besides," boasted an ad for the newly-built Woodruff Apartments in 1908.[5] The Salt Lake buildings were designed either as walk-ups with one or two entrances on each landing, or as a double-loaded corridor with multiple entrances along a central hall. They included decorative brick or stone exteriors and ornate front doorways.

"There's always somebody home in an apartment," advertised the Apartment House Association of Utah. "It's nice to

This 1908 photograph shows a "disappearing" Murphy bed in the interior of the new Woodruff Apartment building. During the day the bed could fold into the wall and the room could be used as a dining area or study. Note the velvet curtains and leaded glass sideboard. Courtesy Utah State Historical Collection, MSS C-275, #09969, Shipler Collection.

return at night to well-lighted corridors and know that help if needed can be quietly summoned."[6] Apartment buildings included a built-in set of comrades who were available to help unclog a sink, lend a cup of sugar, or just give a word of encouragement.[7]

A turn-of-the-century Salt Lake apartment could also be the site of life's dramatic events. Births occurred in the bedrooms. Tonsils were taken out by local doctors on the kitchen table. Deaths occurred in the quiet of the night. Fights broke out into the hallways, where all the residents unwittingly shared in the combat zone. Without much privacy in the tight quarters, messy human interactions spilled over to affect all residents.

Even the names of these historic apartment buildings were a bold statement designed to grab attention and evoke drama. Some were named with exotic European references, such as the Piccardy, the La France, the Marquette, or the Normandy. Others were named after characters in literature, such as Lorna Doone (from an 1869 British novel) or Barbara Worth (from a 1911

This 1908 photograph of an apartment in the Smith Apartments is lavishly furnished with velvet upholstery, lace curtains and an elegant chandelier. The "disappearing" bed is hidden behind the two sets of doors in the cabinet on the wall. Courtesy Utah State Historical Collection, MSS C-275, #08864, Shipler Collection.

American novel). The most common type of building name used a familiar surname, such as Bigelow, Woodruff, Stratton, Ruby, or Sampson. A few were just plain invented, such as the Bell Wines or the Armista. The idea of living in a building with a name is audacious enough, because it is designed to build a sense of collective elegance and exclusivity.[8]

On the stage of your own apartment, you might see the next act of your life come into view. A woman could move in single and move out married. An elderly couple may move in for the last few years of life, and a lonely widow may remain. A nervous high school graduate could find himself launched in his new profession while living at the building. Newlyweds moved in, only to become parents and need a single family home. Then, the apartment stood vacant, awaiting another tenant to begin the reinvention again.

At the beginning of the 20th century, interest in downtown living was at a peak. A 1902 *Salt Lake Tribune* article noted that, "Most of the available sites for houses within convenient distance of the business center are already occupied, and the constant demand of renters for apartments close in has resulted in stimulating the erection of terraces or flats."[9] The population of Salt Lake City increased dramatically from 20,000 residents in the 1880s to more than 92,000 by 1910.[10] By 1940 it had jumped again, to 140,000.[11] This was a time of civic improvements in the inner city, including streetcar lines, paved sidewalks and grass medians in the middle of the wide streets. Downtown apartment living offered the advantages of convenience, comfort and proximity to jobs.

The investors that established Salt Lake's apartments in this period included local families such as the Coveys, Downings, and Sampsons, along with out-of-town financiers from California and surrounding states. There were several prominent builders involved in the apartment construction. W.C.A. (Andy) Vissing, who built more than twenty of the buildings, is credited with the La France, Hillcrest, Kensington, Buckingham, Fairmont and Commander apartments. He came to Salt Lake City from Denmark as a 14-year-old in 1888, married a Covey daughter, formed a construction company and erected many of Salt Lake's enduring edifices.[12] Other examples of apartment contractors were Herrick and Company (Armista), Bowers Investment Company (Piccardy, Lorna Doone, Annie Laurie) and Bettilyon Home Builders (Arlington and Kenneth).

This advertisement for The Woodruff apartment building urges residents to enjoy the many amenities of apartment living and notes that there are even "a number of apartments suitable for bachelors" although references are required. Goodwin's Weekly, September 5, 1908, Utah Digital Newspapers.com

The rental rates for the city's apartments remained relatively stable during most of the early century, starting in the $20 to $30 per month range and increasing to $40 or $50 per month by the mid-century. An interesting scuffle ensued between owners and tenants shortly after World War I, when apartments were in high demand and owners decided to increase rents. "The poor, unfortunate, somewhat misguided and much to be pitied apartment house dweller is facing a dilemma. A regular, full-fledged dilemma with complexities and all the trimmings…The poor fellow – despite impending rental advances – can neither kick nor move. There isn't a vacant apartment in town," reported the *Salt Lake Herald* on August 8, 1919.[13] The Coveys started the rent increases, but other apartment owners quickly followed suit. The Coveys published vehement denials of profiteering and claimed increased costs. New apartment buildings sprung up all through the 1920s and the competitive market resolved the rent dilemma.

Salt Lake City's apartments were constructed in two general phases, with one boom from 1904 through the start of World War I, and then another flurry from the early 1920s until World War II. During the Depression, funding for new construction evaporated. After the War, residents demanded cozy bungalows in the suburbs, which were suddenly more affordable with federally-subsidized loans. Downtown apartment construction declined further, and the patterns of occupancy changed dramatically. The clientele became more transient and less middle class. The buildings became more expensive to maintain. Residents valued different amenities, such as yards and garages, and the charm of apartment living ebbed.

By the early 21st Century, some of these grand old buildings have become upscale condominiums and others serve as low-income or affordable housing. Owners take care to maintain the unique architectural features and advertise the historic beauty of the structures. There are at least 73 of these downtown apartment buildings listed in the National Register of Historic Places.[14] Salt Lake City adopted Design Guidelines for Historic Apartment buildings in 2014, emphasizing their charm as well as their "distinctive urban scale and presence."[15] The more than 100 historic apartment buildings still in use today are a vivid demonstration of the boldness and style with which Salt Lake City entered the 20th Century.

ENDNOTES

1. Interview with Ralph Holding, November 15, 2014.

2. Roger Roper, "Homemakers in Transition: Women in Salt Lake City Apartments, 1910-1940", <u>Utah Historical Quarterly</u>, Vol. 67, No.4, Fall,1999.

3. William Lawrence Murphy invented the disappearing bed in the late 19th century while living in a one-room apartment in San Francisco. He was a gentleman who did not want to court a lady in his bedroom, so he came up with a way to stow his bed in the closet, converting the space into a sitting room. His design was patented in 1911 and became popular for apartment living. "Curator Finds Murphy Bed's Place in American History", by Joseph Caputo, <u>Smithsonian Magazine</u>, April 28, 2009, www.smithsonian.com.

4. Design Guidelines for Historic Apartment & Multifamily Buildings in Salt Lake City, S4:4 PART I, Historic Overview of Apartment and Other Multifamily Buildings; Thomas Carter and Peter Goss. <u>Utah's Historic Architecture</u>, 1847-1940, Salt Lake City, Utah: University of Utah and Utah State Historical Society, 1988.

5. *Goodwin's Weekly*, September 9, 1908.

6. "Live the Apartment Way," *Salt Lake Telegram*, August 29, 1939.

7. Even today, that sense of community within a community exists. I was struck by this as I photographed one building, and saw an elderly lady sitting on the apartment stoop. A young man came out of the building and greeted her: "Hi, Miss Nancy! I got a job interview today, Miss Nancy!" he said. "You'll do well, sugar, you'll do well," she murmured as he flew down the stairs and jumped into his car.

8. Elizabeth Collins Cromley, <u>Alone Together: A History of New York's Early Apartments</u>, Cornell University Press, 1990.

9. *Salt Lake Tribune*, July 27, 1902.

10. "Urban Apartment Buildings," National Register of Historic Places, Multiple Property Documentation Form, Historic Resources of Salt Lake City, Urban Expansion into the Early Twentieth Century, 1890s-1930s, September 12, 1989.

11. Design Guidelines, *ibid*.

12. "Prominent City Contractor Dies," *Salt Lake Tribune*, March 20, 1936.

13. "Rent Raise Called 'Unjustifiable' by Dwellers at Covey," *Salt Lake Herald*, August 8, 1919.

14. "Urban Apartment Buildings," National Register of Historic Places, Multiple Property Documentation Form, Historic Resources of Salt Lake City, Urban Expansion into the Early Twentieth Century, 1890s-1930s, September 12, 1989.

15. Design Guidelines, *ibid*.

SECTION ONE
Bold Beginnings

IN THE EARLY PHASE OF APARTMENT BUILDING before World War I, the most common design was the "walk-up" plan with six units. Each three- or four-story building had a central entrance with two apartments opening off the landing. Units were known for their extensive front porches, often with columns and decorative railings. Colonial Revival or Neo-Classical architectural styles were popular.

PAULINE | 1904 | 278 EAST 100 SOUTH

Note the cut sandstone foundation, iron railing balconies, Colonial Revival styling. Later expanded to the south and renamed "The Progress Apartments."

SMITH | 1908 | 228 SOUTH 300 EAST

DESIGNED BY WARE AND TREGANZA, in the Prairie School style.

LA FRANCE | 1905 | 246 WEST 300 SOUTH

BUILT BY THE COVEY BROTHERS as the first of many developments in the city, called "The Covey Flats" until another building was built named "The Covey Apartments". Contractor was W.C.A. "Andy" Vissing who built at least 20 apartment buildings in Salt Lake. Note the iron lobby railing, the apartment courts behind the main building and the walk-up design.

ALTADENA | 1906 | SOUTH 300 EAST

Both the Altadena and Sampson buildings on this corner were built by the Octavius Sampson family. Octavius was a British immigrant who built a fortune in the sheep industry. He and his family lived in the building as managers at various times. The Altadena was originally Sampson Flats but the name was changed to Altadena to honor the Sampsons' newborn daughter in 1907. Note the Neo-Classical features such as pedimented entrances, keystones above the windows and columns. The Altadena originally had an exterior elevator, unusual for the time period.

SAMPSON | 1906 | 276 EAST 300 SOUTH

Two sisters lived in Unit H at the Altadena in the 1950s: Annette and Martha Rustad. Both were Norwegian immigrants who worked as seamstresses and tailors for downtown clothing stores such as Auerbach's and Keith O'Brien. They became naturalized citizens on May 5, 1921. According to census records, neither sister was married nor had children. They died in 1968 and are buried next to each other in the Salt Lake City Cemetery.

WOODRUFF | 1908 | 235 SOUTH 200 EAST

Advertised to "young men looking for desirable apartments close to their work" who would enjoy the café on the premises. Other features included steam heat, hot water, telephone, janitor, night watchman and the walls could be "tinted to suit the taste of the tenant." Note the light posts once at the entrance.

Abraham Gross and his young family lived in the Woodruff from 1930 to 1935. Abe and his wife, Vera, were born in Poland and immigrated to the United States at the end of World War I. In 1928 they moved to Salt Lake City from Chicago, where Abe learned his trade as a truck driver and cattle buyer. They spoke Polish and English in their home. The couple started their family living at unit 60 in the Woodruff while their son, Jerome, was born. On September 19, 1935 Abe was on a cattle-buying trip near Pleasant Grove and was killed driving across the train tracks. Abe is buried in the Jewish section of the Salt Lake City cemetery. Vera was left a widow with two-year-old Jerome and moved from the Woodruff later that year. Unit 60 remained vacant for two years after the tragedy.

MARQUETTE | 1909 | 569 EAST 300 SOUTH

CAITHNESS - RITER | 1908 | 86 B STREET

Designed by Ware and Treganza. Note the unusually-colored brick, the clinker brick style and the beautiful stained, leaded-glass windows.

IVANHOE | 1908 | 417 EAST 300 SOUTH

OQUIRRH | 1908 | 325 S 400 E

SILVERADO | 1906 | 243 S 300 E

GIBBONS | 1908 | 251 E 300 S

NELSON | 1909 | 347 S 300 E

HOLLYWOOD | 1909 | 284 EAST 100 SOUTH

BUNGALOW | 1909 | 15 SOUTH 300 EAST

COLONIAL | 1907 | 460 E 300 S

RAINIER | 1908 | 215 S 300 E

CORNELL | 1910 | 101 S 600 E

PALACE | 1911 | 145 S 300 E

RUBY | 1912 | 435 EAST 200 SOUTH

Built at the end of the early phase prior to World War I, with 21 walk-up units and beautiful wood-framed doors and windows.

Dressmaker Sadie Baldwin lived in the Ruby as a single mother in the 1920s. She was the daughter of Swedish immigrants and had only an 8th grade education but earned $720 per year as a dressmaker in her own shop. She lived in Unit 1 with her daughter, Larue, and her son, Thomas.

PRINCETON - BOULEVARD | 1915 | 100 SOUTH 900 EAST
BUILT BY W.C.A. "ANDY" VISSING.

VERNON-ERVIN RAY | 1913 | 480 EAST 300 SOUTH

ELISE | 1914 | 561 EAST 100 SOUTH

Note the large columns, different iron railings on each balcony, and double windows lighting the center stairway.

COVEY | 1909 | 239 EAST SOUTH TEMPLE

The most luxurious of the Covey buildings, with a passenger elevator serving seven stories. The Covey brothers – Almon Andrew ("A.A."), Hyrum Theron ("H.T.") and Stephen Mack ("S.M.") – were a successful group of investors, contractors, ranchers and entrepreneurs who built several of Salt Lake City's largest apartment complexes during the early 20th Century. They originally made their fortune herding sheep in Wyoming, but also had investments in oil and real estate. Beyond apartments, they owned the Little America motels and gas stations, the Rainbow Rendezvous dance hall and Ballard-Covey Motors. After their original apartment building – the La France on 300 South – succeeded, they built several high-end developments from South Temple to the lower Avenues: the Kensington, Hillcrest, New Hillcrest and Buckingham.

KENSINGTON | 1906 | 180 NORTH MAIN

An antique postcard showing the early Covey buildings. On the reverse side of the postcard it notes: "Covey Investment Company – Owner and Operator of 350 of Salt Lake City's Finest Apartments – 2 to 6 rooms – furnished and unfurnished. Garages in Connection."

Eugene and Reva Holding managed the Hillcrest Apartments from 1922-1954, living first in unit A and then unit 2. Their sons, Ralph and Earl, were each born in the apartment's bedroom with a midwife in attendance. Ralph remembers having his tonsils taken out by a doctor who operated on the kitchen table while Ralph was doused with ether. Because their unit was only two bedrooms, the boys shared a glassed-in sleeping porch while their older sister used one bedroom and the parents used the other. Their kitchen had an icebox supplied by regular deliveries from the iceman, until they were upgraded to Frigidaire units supplied from a central compressor in the basement. They also had a gas range for a monthly charge of $1.

Managing an apartment building in the early 20th century involved being a jack-of-all trades. For the Holding couple, their duties included collecting rents, removing snow on all sidewalks and even into the street to clear parking spaces, vacuuming hallway carpets weekly, mopping and shining entry floors weekly, taking out the garbage from each unit daily (both a "wet" and a "dry" can), cleaning the wallpaper every spring in each unit, repainting and refinishing the hardwood floors when a tenant moved out, and making all repairs for tenants. The manager had a key to every unit in a lockbox to help anyone who was locked out, day or night. One of the more difficult tasks involved climbing up in the attic of each building in the spring and fall to open or close the roof vents and get cross-ventilation, because the buildings had no air conditioning and needed the cool City Creek Canyon breezes.

"There were laundry rooms in the basement, where a washing machine did your load for a quarter," Ralph recalls, "and we even had dryers – the type with vertical drawers that pulled out and you hung your clothes on them to dry." The Covey owners insisted on having beautiful flower gardens around each building that needed to be planted twice each year. "My dad would walk around the gardens at Temple Square and Liberty Park each year with the building owner, H.T. Covey, and then they would decide what to plant at the Hillcrest," Ralph said. The beds would be planted in the spring with geraniums, lilies and other annuals, then changed to bulbs each fall. When World War II started, all available men including Ralph were called into the service, so the Holdings' teenaged son, Earl, became the gardener and assistant custodian for the buildings. The Hillcrest was decorated at Christmas with a sleigh and reindeer across the roof. Tenants usually stayed at the Hillcrest for many years, Ralph noted, because it was so convenient to have a grocery store, pharmacy and garage across the street and two streetcar lines running right in front of the building.

HILLCREST | 1915 | 155 FIRST AVENUE

NEW HILLCREST | 1918 | 87 A STREET

BUCKINGHAM | 1916 | 241 EAST SOUTH TEMPLE

SECTION TWO
Building Boom

During the heady days of the 1920s, Salt Lake City's apartments multiplied by several new buildings constructed each year. The designs changed from "walk-up" plans to "double-loaded corridor" plans to pack more units into each building footprint. Residents entered individual units from a main hallway and shared common walls on both sides of the apartment. Although front porches largely disappeared, some buildings still featured balconies. The long narrow shape of the plan is well-suited to Salt Lake City's deep square blocks.

QUINN-MALO | 1923 | 279 SOUTH 700 EAST

CLAIRMONT | 1923 | 446 E 300 S   LINCOLN ARMS | 1924 | 242 E 100 S

DENI-ZAY | 1925 | 254 S 300 E

BREELYN – RIGBY | 1925 | 435 E 100 S

MAHDEEN | 1925 | 47 S 300 E

ASHBY - SUZANNE | 1925 | 358 E 100 S

ARMISTA | 1927 | 555 EAST 100 SOUTH

BUILT BY HERRICK AND COMPANY, featuring a solid Colonial Revival style and a double-loaded corridor plan with 30 units. The name was later changed to the Waldorf Apartments. A *Salt Lake Tribune* ad in October 16, 1927 read: "Splendid 3 room apartments equipped with electric ranges and electric refrigeration. $40.00 to $42.00. One of the most modernly equipped and conveniently located apartments in the city."

Prominent Utahn Noble Warrum, Jr. lived here in 1931. He was a lawyer, newspaper editor, U.S. Postmaster and diplomat. In 1895, Warrum was a signer of the original Utah State Constitution. He and his wife, Julia, lived in Mexico during the 1920s and 1930s where he worked at the consulate. Upon returning to Utah, they moved to the luxurious Armista.

EMBASSY | 1926 | 130 SOUTH 300 EAST

The Embassy, Embassy Arms and Downing DeLuxe buildings along 300 East were all built by investors Bessie P. and Hardy K. Downing. Hardy Downing worked as a cowboy, athlete and tandem bike racer at the turn of the century. Hardy liked to say he was "in the bicycle game," traveling as far as Australia and Europe to ride the circuit. He held the mile tandem record with Vic Benson for many years. Hardy and Bessie served as on-site managers of their buildings during the 1930s and 1940s, raising their family of four children.

TRENTON | 1927 | 544 E 100 S

SPENCER STEWART | 1926 | 740 E 300 S

A simply-styled building using a double-loaded corridor plan with 29 units. A 1935 *Salt Lake Telegram* ad read: "Spencer Stewart Apartments: three rooms, electric refrigerator and range, furnished or unfurnished, disappearing beds, nice large rooms, moderate rent."

BELL WINES | 1927 | 530 EAST 100 SOUTH

Built in an unusual style with a corner plan and a center porch evocative of antebellum southern mansions. The name comes from combining the owners' surnames – Hazel Bell and Stanley J. Wines. They married in Nevada in 1907 and had five children. At the time they built the Bell Wines, they were spending time in both Utah and Nevada, where Stanley worked in a mine. They lost ownership of the building during the Depression and moved to Reno. Stanley became a contractor while Hazel was elected to the State Legislature.

Eva Harmer was a 22-year-old single woman when she lived in the Bell Wines in 1934. She fell in love with Blaine Allan of Springville. They became engaged in August, 1934, but Eva dropped her $250 engagement ring down the apartment's sink. The plumber couldn't find it, so the city workers went down the manhole in the street, stretched a net across the pipe, and waited for the ring to appear. Two days later it was safely back on Eva's finger. She and Blaine were married in November, moved to Heber and raised eight children while Blaine taught school.

WESTCLIFF | 1927 | 419 E 200 S

EASTCLIFF | 1926 | 425 E 200 S

CLARENDON | 1927 | 53 S 300 E

BENWORTH | 1927 | 227 S 400 E

MAYFLOWER | 1929 | 1283 EAST SOUTH TEMPLE

Designed by famous Utah architect, Slack Winburn, who attended the Ecole des Beaux Arts in Paris and also designed the Elaine apartments, the Clift Building and the Memory Grove Park entry gates. The building is similar to a Manhattan co-op, with five floors featuring only four large apartments on each floor. The apartments range from 2,000-2,400 square feet, with rich woodwork, fireplaces, formal entries and butler's pantries.

Charlotte Garff Jacobsen remembers visiting her grandparents, Eric W. and Charlotte Critchlow Ryberg, who lived in the Mayflower from the 1940s through Mrs. Ryberg's death in 1976. "Grandma lived on the fifth floor in #501, the southeast corner. Her front windows were French doors…Grandma's was especially light and open feeling being on the top floor." Her family gathered at the Mayflower every Christmas Eve: "Grandma would sit at her beautiful dining room table…and we would eat like royalty…One of my favorite things to do on Christmas Eve was stand in front of her French doors on the front of her living room and watch the traffic come down 1300 East. It was especially beautiful if it was also snowing. I also loved riding the elevator, which had a door with a small window and a gate you stepped through." Charlotte's grandmother planted and tended the rose garden that can still be enjoyed on the west side of the building.

MAYFLOWER

VILLA ANDREA | 1927 | 265 EAST FIRST AVENUE

Built with unique Italianate styling by the Catholic diocese to house nuns working at the nearby Cathedral of the Madeleine.

GRAYLYNN | 1929 | 205 EAST SECOND AVENUE

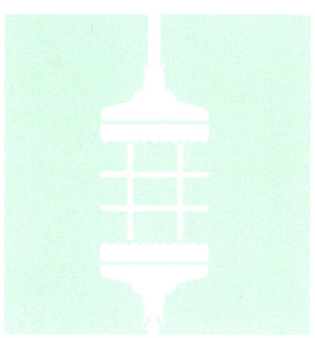

SECTION THREE
Dramatic Designs

The builders added many interesting details to the architecture of the early Salt Lake City apartment buildings, often using Period Revival styles and elements. The timbering details of the English Tudor, the steep roof gables and parapets of the Jacobethan themes, and the horsehoe arches and geometric shapes of the Moorish styles are all in evidence. The entrances, with their dramatic doorways and prominent signs, are especially charming.

PETER PAN | 1927 | 445 EAST 300 SOUTH

Note the tile roofs, the variety of brick colors and the delightful neon sign.

Ila Marr Seely, 33, lived at the Peter Pan in 1941. She was a single woman working as a secretary for the National Youth Administration earning $1,352 per year. Ila grew up in East Millcreek but moved downtown for an adventure. In 1939 she was reported dead by her brothers, who identified her body as a car accident victim. An early morning crash on the Midvale-Bingham Highway took the lives of a young man and woman, but the brothers mistook the woman's corpse as that of their sister. Ila later appeared in person to contradict their report.

LORNA DOONE | 1928 | 320 EAST 100 SOUTH

BUILT AS PART OF A LARGE COMPLEX that afforded a common interior block parking lot. The sister buildings of Lorna Doone and adjacent Annie Laurie were built by Bowers Development Company. Each building contains 30 units and cost $80,000 to build.

ANNIE LAURIE | 1928 | 326 EAST 100 SOUTH

Note the elaborate gothic gargoyles at the entrance and on the roofline. They originally featured intricate glass doors under the stone archways. The name "Lorna Doone" refers to an 1869 British novel made into a film about a woman who discovers she is an heiress. The name "Annie Laurie" comes from a Scottish folk song.

Maude Karren Richards began living at unit 201 in the Lorna Doone in 1932 with her husband, Fred Richards. Earlier, Fred had been a barber in his own shop, but illness forced him to quit and Maude was supporting the family by managing the apartments. Fred died the next year at the age of 44, leaving Maude a widow for the rest of her life. She lived in and managed several downtown Salt Lake apartment buildings, including the Castle Heights. She also worked as the Jail Matron at the Salt Lake County Jail. It was reported in the August 13, 1949 *Salt Lake Tribune* that Maude was widely remembered by her ex-wards on holidays: "'I've accumulated a wonderful group of my friends through my contacts with women placed in my care,' Mrs. Richards told the paper, 'and that's the best part of my job.' During 13 years of caring for all types of women – slayers, bandits, narcotic violators, and other criminals -- Mrs. Richards said not once has she been subjected to vulgar language or violence of any type, except from a few mental patients… 'Do I like my job? Well, certainly. I wouldn't trade it for anything. I love my fan mail, too,' she said enthusiastically."

ELAINE | 1928 | 440 EAST 300 SOUTH

DESIGNED BY WELL-KNOWN UTAH ARCHITECT SLACK WINBURN and distinctive for its lovely courtyard garden.

VANNAS | 1930 | 121 SOUTH 600 EAST

LOS GABLES | 1929 | 135 SOUTH 300 EAST

One of the largest of the buildings with 80 units. It features lovely stone work at the street level, Moorish arched entrances and timbering detail around some of the upper windows. Also called "The Caledonian."

Young married couple Larry and Rosalee Hunt lived at the Los Gables in 1959. They were originally from St. George but when Larry served in the Army he was assigned to Fort Douglas and they needed a place to live with their newborn daughter. After staying with relatives a short time they rented Unit 605 at the Los Gables and lived there six months. The building advertised itself as "an address to be proud of" with "reasonable monthly rents."

PICCADILLY | 1929 | 24 SOUTH 500 EAST

BIGELOW | 1930 | 223 SOUTH 400 EAST

There are 30 units in this double-loaded corridor plan and apartments. According to a 1940 newspaper ad, they rented for $33.50 per month: "2 rm modern, lots of space, light, all electric, good service, exclusive."

EMBASSY ARMS | 1930 | 120 SOUTH 300 EAST

This building has the most elegant style of the Downing group, with its French Door balconies, intricate brick patterns and glowing neon sign. Residents in 1951 included Royal J. Harris and his wife, Angela, who moved here after he retired from the plumbing trade.

OXFORD – DEL ROYA | 1930 | 334 EAST 300 SOUTH

PICCARDY | 1930 | 115 SOUTH 300 EAST

BUILT IN A JACOBETHAN REVIVAL STYLE with an entrance featuring twisting columns and composite capitols supporting a cornice with brackets and large finials. The central hallway windows have leaded glass and the entrance has mosaic tile. Each apartment originally had dairyman delivery access doors. Some units have vestiges of the original Murphy beds within glazed French Door closets.

SECTION FOUR
Elegant to the End

SOME OF THE MOST CREATIVE AND FLAMBOYANT APARTMENT DESIGNS came during the grand era of apartment building before the Great Depression. Flourishes such as stonework, gargoyles and castellated roofs adorned the exteriors, while interior entrances added tile, marble and chandeliers. As the initial wave of early apartment building came to a close, the emphasis was on charm.

PREMIER | 1931 | 27 SOUTH 800 EAST

This 18-unit complex was built for $50,000 on a unusually large lot set back from the street. Note the courtyard with stone detail around the doorways and the wrought iron sign on the roof.

Western Air Express pilot Ray F. Ellinghouse lived at the Premier from 1941-1944 with his wife, Ethel, and their son, Jerry. Ray and Ethel moved from Montana to Salt Lake City in 1935 to pursue his flying career. Ray was earning a generous annual salary of $2,600 piloting passenger planes to West Yellowstone. In 1946 he made headlines when he witnessed a mid-air crash at Salt Lake Airport that killed a young student pilot. Ray helped investigate the crash.

FONTENELLE | 153 EAST SECOND AVENUE

STRATTON | 1927 | 49 SOUTH 400 EAST

The arches over the balcony windows and the ornamentation on the roofline add elegance to this simple façade. The entrance with the arched door and windows is also lovely.

In 1940, residents of the Stratton included Ridgely W. Powell, 32, his wife, Kathleen, 32, and their 5-year-old son Ridgely, Jr., originally from Oregon. Ridgely worked at a Salt Lake bank earning $1,680 per year and Kathleen worked at Utah Power and Light operating a calculator for $1,070 per year. Both were college graduates. Other residents here included young couples with one or two children, often employed as seamstresses, truck drivers, patrolmen and file clerks.

CHATEAU NORMANDIE - MOYLE | 1931 | 63 SOUTH 400 EAST

One of the last walk-up apartment buildings built in Salt Lake City's first wave of apartments. It features dramatic Period Revival style with timbering and an impressive tile entrance.

BARBARA WORTH | 1931 | 326 EAST SOUTH TEMPLE

BUILT BY GRAHAM AND LEONE DOXEY along with their real estate partners, Howard and Leone Layton. The partnership lasted for several generations. The building is in the Tudor Revival style with striking window details and timbering. Interiors have arched doorways and hardwood floors. An April 14, 1940 *Salt Lake Telegram* ad read: "Barbara Worth: delightful front 3 rm apt., living room, 14 x 24, de luxe features, reasonable rent."

CHAPEL HILL | 1910 | 454 EAST THIRD AVENUE

KNICKERBOCKER | 1912 | 1280 EAST SOUTH TEMPLE

CASTLE HEIGHTS | 1931 | 141 EAST FIRST AVENUE

MARYLAND | 1912 | 839 E SOUTH TEMPLE

THIS BUILDING IS ONE OF THE MOST ORNATE APARTMENT BUILDINGS in downtown, known for its stone work and large balconies. The Utah Heritage Foundation brochure notes: "The exuberant, exaggerated ornamentation of this Neo-Classical building gives it a heavy feel. The large cornice features modillion brackets above egg-and-dart and dentil moldings." Slack Winburn was the architect. George and Frank Bowers, of the Bowers Building Company, built it for Bernard O. Mecklenburg, who originally named the apartments after himself. Mecklenburg was a Nebraska native who came to Salt Lake to work on the Cathedral of the Madeleine. He changed the building name to the "Maryland Apartments" in 1917, possibly to avoid association with his German heritage during World War I.

ARLINGTON | 415 E First Ave

BEVERLY | 45 S 700 E

BRIAR ARMS | 335 S 200 E

COMMANDER | 1928 | 125 S 1300 E

COMMODORE | 1107 E S Temple

COUNCIL CREST | 706 E 300 S

CRITCHLOW | 379 E First Ave

HILLVIEW | 1911 | 1272 E 200 S

DORIUS | 1910 | 553 E First Ave

DRAYTON | 1211 E First Ave

EDGEHILL | 227 S 1300 E

EMMA | 1907 | 1119 E First Ave

FEDERAL HEIGHTS | 1321 E S Temple

KEARNS | 1926 | 250 S 500 E

LA SELLE | 300 S 500 E

LUND | 1911 | 135 S 700 E

MCCULLOUGH | 125 S 600 E

MEREDITH | 170 E First Ave

PEERY | 1911 | 223 E Third Ave

PETER JR. | 1925 | 35 S 700 E

POLLYANNA | 35 F Street

RITZ | 35 E South Temple

SCARSDALE | 1931 | 125 S 900 E

STANTON | 146 E Second Ave

SWALLOW | 333 E 100 S

VIVA | 1927 | 150 S 700 E

WESLEY | 217 E Third Ave

56 S 1300 E

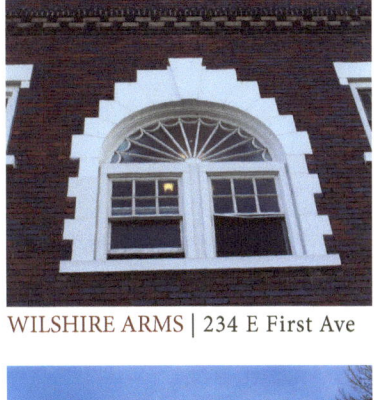
WILSHIRE ARMS | 234 E First Ave

162 I Street

YALE | 144 E Second Ave

800 E 300 S

MAP

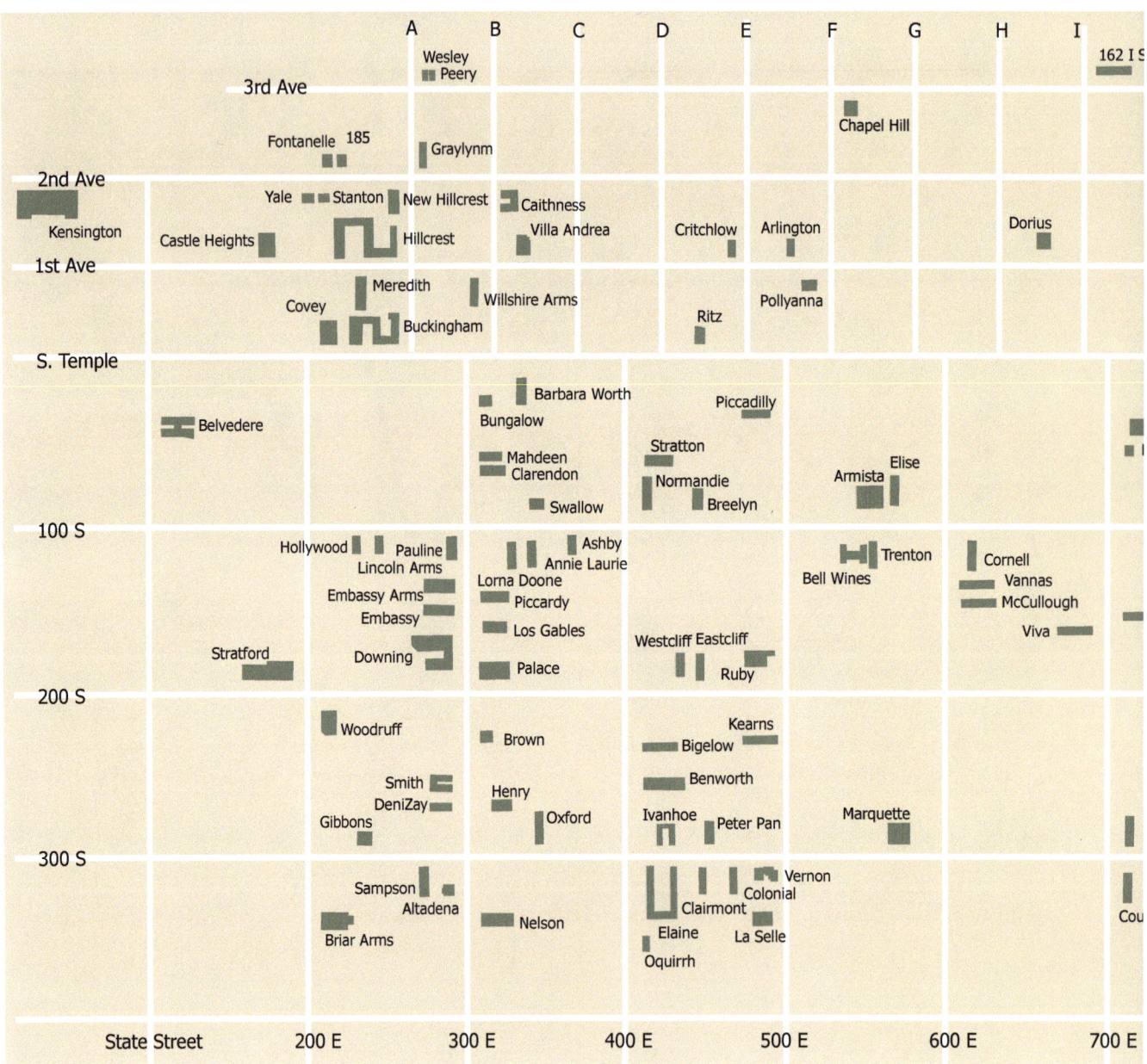

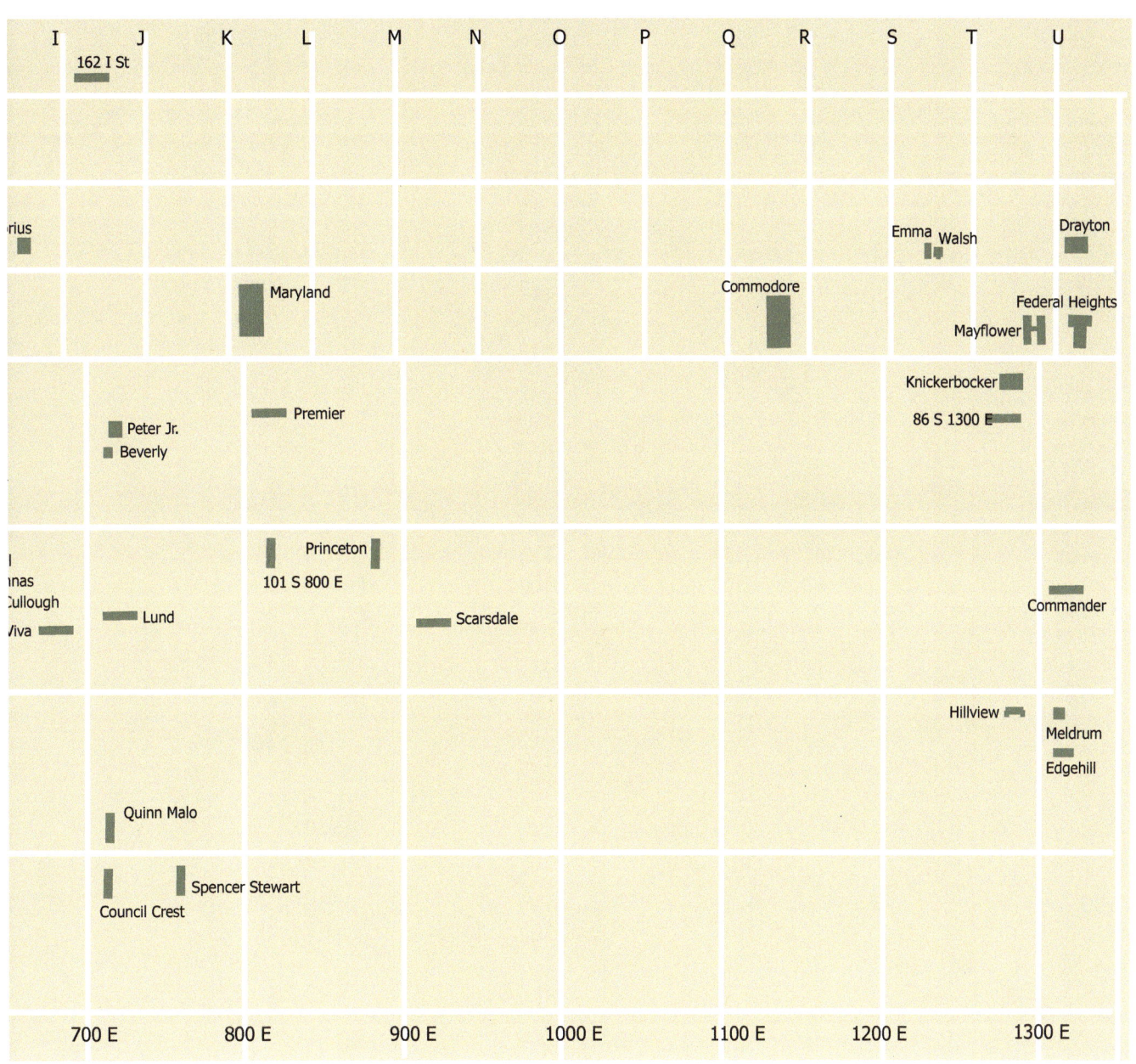

MAP LIST

Salt Lake City Historic Apartments Still Standing as of 6/4/2016

Name	Address	Year
Altadena	310 S 300 E	1906
Annie Laurie	326 E 100 S	1928
Arlington	415 First Ave	
Armista	555 E 100 S	1927
Ashby - Suzanne	358 E 100 S	1925
Barbara Worth	326 E S Temple	1931
Bell Wines	530 E 100 S	1927
Belvedere	29 S State	1919
Benworth - Chapman	227 S 400 E	1927
Beverly	45 S 700 E	
Bigelow	223 S 400 E	1930
Breelyn - Rigby	435 E 100 S	1925
Brown - Rainier	215 S 300 E	1908
Buckingham	245 E S Temple	1915
Bungalow	15 S 300 E	1909
Caithness	86 B	1909
Castle Heights	141 First Ave	1931
Chapel Hill	454 Third Ave	
Chateau Normandie	63 S 400 E	1931
Clairmont	446 E 300 S	1923
Clarendon	53 S 300 E	1927
Colonial - Glenwood	460 E 200 S	1910
Commander	125 S 1300 E	1929
Commodore	1107 S Temple	
Cornell	101 S 600 E	1910
Corona - Briar Arms	335 S 200 E	1925
Council Crest	706 E 300 S	
Covey	239 E S Temple	1909
Critchlow	379 First Ave	1908
Del Roya - Oxford	334 E 300 S	1930
Deni Zay	254 S 300 E	1925
Dorius	553 First Ave	1910
Downing	136 S 300 E	1922
Drayton	1211 First Ave	1910
Eastcliff -Cummings	422 E 200 S	1926
Edgehill - Wasatch	227 S 1300 E	1925
Eighth East	101 S 800 E	
Elaine	440 E 300 S	1928
Elise	561 E 100 S	1914
Embassy Arms	120 S 300 E	1930
Embassy	130 S 300 E	1926
Emma	1119 First Ave	1907
Federal Heights	1321 E S Temple	1930
Fontenelle	153 Second Ave	
Graylynn	205 Second Ave	1929
Gibbons - Eden	251 E 300 S	1908
Henry - Silverado	243 S 300 E	1906
Hillcrest	155 First Ave	1925
Hillview - Cluff	1272-76 E 200 S	1911
Hollywood	234 E 100 S	1909
Ivanhoe	417 E 300 S	1908
Kearns	250 S 500 E	1926
Kensington	180 N Main	1906
Knickerbocker	1280 E S Temple	1912
La Selle	300 S 500 E	
Lincoln Arms	242 E 100 S	1924
Lorna Doone	320 E 100 S	1928
Lund	135 S 700 E	1909
Los Gables	135 S 300 E	1929
Mahdeen	47 S 300 E	1925
Marquette	569 E 300 S	1909
Maryland	839 E S Temple	1912
Mayflower	1283 E S Temple	1929
McCullough	125 S 600 E	1928
Meredith	170 First Ave	1915
Nelson	347 S 300 E	1909
New Hillcrest	A St/Second Ave	
Oquirrh	325 S 400 E	1908
Palace	145 S 300 E	1911
Pauline	278 E 100 S	1904
Peery	223 Third Ave	1911
Peter Pan	445 E 300 S	1927
Peter Jr.	35 S 700 E	1925
Piccadilly	24 S 500 E	1929
Piccardy	115 S 300 E	1930
Pollyanna	35 F	
Premier	27 S 800 E	1931
Princeton - Boulevard	870 E 100 S	1911

Name	Address	Year
Quinn Malo	279 S 700 E	1923
Ritz	435 E S Temple	
Ruby	435 E 200 S	1912
Sampson	276 E 300 S	1906
Scarsdale - Beezley	125 S 900 E	1931
Smith	228 S 300 E	1908
Spencer Stewart	740 E 300 S	1926
Stanton	146 Second Ave	
Stratford	169 E 200 S	
Stratton	49 S 400 E	1927
Swallow	333 E 100 S	
Trenton	544 E 100 S	1927
University - Meldrum	201 S 1300 E	1907
Vannas	121 S 600 E	1930
Vernon -Ervin Ray	480 E 300 S	1913
Villa Andrea	265 First Ave	1927
Viva	150 S 700 E	1927
Walsh	1135 First Ave	
Wesley	217 Third Ave	1911
Westcliff - Cummings	419 E 200 S	1927
Wilshire Arms	234 First Ave	
Woodruff	235 S 200 E	1908
Yale	144 Second Ave	

INDEX

Allan, Blaine	59
Altadena	24-25
Annie Laurie	14, 71
Arlington	14, 98
Armista	14, 55
Ashby – Suzanne	54
Baldwin, Sadie	36
Barbara Worth	13, 90
Bell Wines	14, 58-59
Bell, Hazel	59
Benworth – Chapman	60
Beverly	98
Bigelow	13, 77
Bowers, Frank	96
Bowers, George	96
Breelyn - Rigby	54
Brown - Rainier	35
Buckingham	14, 43, 49
Bungalow	34
Caithness- Riter	29
Castle Heights	71, 94-95
Chapel Hill	91
Chateau Normandie	88-89
Clairmont	53
Clarendon	60
Colonial – Glenwood	35
Commander	14, 98
Commodore	98
Cornell	35
Corona - Briar Arms	98
Council Crest	9, 98
Covey	23, 42-43
Covey, Almon Andrew	43
Covey, Hyrum Theron	43, 47
Covey, Stephen Mack	43
Critchlow	98
Del Roya – Oxford	79
Deni Zay	54

Dorius	99
Downing	56, 78
Downing, Hardy K., Bessie P.	56
Doxey, Graham, Leone	90
Drayton	99
Eastcliff - Cummings	60
Edgehill - Wasatch	99
Elaine	61, 72
Elise	40-41
Ellinghouse, Ray F., Ethel	84
Embassy Arms	56, 78
Embassy	50-51, 56
Emma	99
Federal Heights	99
Fontenelle	86
Gibbons – Eden	31
Graylynn	65
Gross, Abraham, Vera	26
Harmer, Eva	59
Harris, Royal J., Angela	78
Henry – Silverado – Winters	31
Herrick and Company	55
Hillcrest	14, 43, 46-47
Hillview - Cluff	98
Holding, Eugene, Reva	46-47
Holding, Ralph	46-47
Holding, Earl	46-47
Hollywood	32-33
Hunt, Larry, Rosalee	74
Ivanhoe	30
Jacobsen, Charlotte Garff	61
Kearns	99
Kensington	14, 43-45
Knickerbocker	92-93

INDEX

La France	13, 22-23, 43
La Selle	99
Layton, Howard, Leone	90
Lincoln Arms	53
Lorna Doone	13, 70-71
Los Gables	9, 74-75
Lund	99
Mahdeen	54
Marquette	13, 28
Maryland	96-97
Mayflower	61-63
McCullough	100
Mecklenburg, Bernard O.	96
Meredith	100
Moyle	88-89
Nelson	31
New Hillcrest	43, 48
Oquirrh	31
Palace	35
Pauline	20
Peery	100
Peter Jr.	100
Peter Pan	11, 66-69
Piccadill	11, 76
Piccardy	13, 80-81
Pollyanna	100
Powell, Ridgely W., Kathleen	87
Premier	82-85
Princeton – Boulevard	38
Quinn – Malo	52
Richards, Fred and Maude Karren	71
Ritz	100
Ruby	14, 36-37
Rustad, Annette and Martha	25
Ryberg, Eric W., Charlotte	61
Sampson	14, 19, 24-25
Sampson, Octavius	24
Scarsdale – Beezley	100
Seely, Ila Marr	69
Smith	13, 20
Spencer Stewart	57
Stanton	100
Stratton	14, 87
Swallow	101
Trenton	57
Vannas	73
Vernon - Ervin Ray	39
Villa Andrea	64
Vissing, W.C.A.	14, 23
Viva	101
Ware and Treganza	21, 29
Warrum, Noble, Julia	55
Wesley	101
Westcliff – Cummings	60
Wilshire Arms	101
Winburn, Slack	61, 72, 96
Wines, Stanley J.	59
Woodruff	11, 12, 14-15, 26-27
Yale	101

SOURCES AND NOTES

In September 12, 1989, historian Roger Roper of the Utah State Historical Society prepared a National Register of Historic Places Nomination form seeking designation for multiple Salt Lake City apartment buildings. The nomination form is a valuable resource for apartment construction dates and other historical context of urbanization. In addition, I used information from individual apartment nomination forms as most of the buildings in this book are listed on the National Register. All those forms can be found online at http://www.nationalregisterofhistoricplaces.com/ut/

The United States Census forms were invaluable in locating information about apartment residents. These records can be found online at www.familysearch.org.

The Polk's Directory books for Salt Lake City, Utah contain a special section on apartment buildings in the city. In that section, the residents of each apartment building are listed in a given year. I used these directories extensively to recreate residence and building histories used herein. The directories are located in the Research Center of Utah State Archives and Utah State History, 300 Rio Grande, Salt Lake City, Utah.

In addition, there were the following sources for information found on the individual pages:

Altadena – The information about the Octavius Sampson comes from U.S. Census records for 1910, 1920, 1930, 1940 and the Polk's Directory for the relevant years.

Sampson – The story about the Rustad sisters comes from the U.S. Census records for 1920, 1930, 1940 and the Polk's Directory for the relevant years.

Woodruff – The quotes from the March 27, 1909 ad for the Woodruff are in a series of ads run in the *Goodwin's Weekly* newspaper during fall, 1908 and spring, 1909, accessed online at www.utahdigitalnewspapers.com. The information about Abraham Gross' fatal accident was found in the *Salt Lake Telegram*, September 14, 1935, "Car Carried Quarter Mile in Collision," *The Pleasant Grove Review*, September 20, 1935, "Union Pacific Train Kills Local Resident," and his Death Certificate online at www.archives.utah.gov, entry number 81448.

Ruby – The story about Sadie Baldwin comes from the U.S. Census records for 1920, 1930 and 1940 along with Polk's Directory for the relevant years.

Hillcrest – During November and December, 2014, the author personally interviewed and corresponded with Ralph Holding, the son of Eugene and Reva Holding, whose story is told in connection with the Hillcrest Apartments.

Armista – The quotes from the ad appeared in the October 16, 1927 *Salt Lake Tribune*. The information about Noble Warrum comes from the U.S. Census records for 1900, 1910, 1920, 1930 and 1940 along with the Polk's Directory for the relevant years and his books, *Utah Since Statehood, Volumes I-IV*, by Noble Warrum, S.J. Clarke Publishing, Chicago and Salt Lake City, 1919.

Embassy – The stories about the Downing family were contained in the "Sports Mirror" column by John Mooney, *Salt Lake Tribune*, July 11, 1960 and an obituary for Hardy Kenneth Downing, Sr. online at www.findagrave.com.

Bell Wines – The information on Stanley and Hazel Bell Wines came from an article at the Nevada Women's History Project, www.umnr.edu/nwhp/gios/women/wines.html, researched and written by Jane Ellsworth Olive and posted to the website February 2011. The story about Eva Harmer's wedding ring was written up in a *Salt Lake Tribune* article, August 16, 1934, page 9.

Mayflower – The Slack Winburn information is found in an article written by Kirk Huffaker entitled "Utah Architect Remembered: Slack Winburn" in the *Utah Preservation* magazine published by the Utah Heritage Foundation, February, 2011, p. 66, available online at http://www.slmodern.org/2011/12/02. The story from Charlotte Garff Jacobsen was told in personal correspondence with the author dated April 11, 2016.

Peter Pan – The Ila Mar Seely story came from census records and an October 19, 1939 *Salt Lake Tribune* article entitled "Overturning Auto Kills Two Salt Lakers, Injures Three Others; Bingham Road Curve Traps Speeding Auto Victims of Early Morning Crash."

Annie Laurie – The story of Maude Karren Richards and her husband, Fred, was documented in a *Salt Lake Tribune* article on August 13, 1949 entitled "Ex-Wards Remember Jail Matron When Christmas Rolls Around – or Easter, or St. Valentine's Day or Most Any Other Special Day" as well as the Death Certificate for Maude Karren Richards dated

Jan 23, 1956, www.sorenson-robey.org, and a *Salt Lake Telegram* article entitled "Funeral Rites Being Planned for S.L. Man" dated July 15, 1931.

Los Gables – The story of Larry and Rosalee Hunt is personal to the author and comes from her family records. The ad reference appears in the Yellow Pages of the *Salt Lake City Classified Telephone Directory* for 1959, page 13 under the "Apartment" category.

Bigelow – The ad appeared in the *Salt Lake Telegram*, April 14, 1940 issue, available online at www.utahdigitalnewspapers.com.

Embassy Arms – The Royal Harris family information came from the online obituaries of Angela Bryan Austin Harris, 1896-1984 at www.findagrave.com and Joshua Royal Harris, 1894-1960 at www.findagrave.com.

Premier – The Ellinghouse data was found in the 1930 and 1940 U.S. Census records. Ray Ellinghouse's assistance with an accident investigation was documented in a *Deseret News* article dated August 28, 1946 and his flying career was detailed in a *Salt Lake Tribune* article dated June 12, 1936 entitled "Parks Plane Starts Yellowstone Service With H.C. "Hank" Hollenbeck and Ray Ellinghouse At the Controls".

Stratton – The 1940 U.S. Census Records were the source for the Powell family story.

Maryland – The information about the Maryland came from the Utah Heritage Foundation brochure on the South Temple Historic District accessed online at www.utahheritagefoundation.com.

BIBLIOGRAPHY

Roger Roper, "Homemakers in Transition: Women in Salt Lake City Apartments, 1910-1940", *Utah Historical Quarterly*, 1999.

Elizabeth Collins Cromley, *Alone Together: A History of New York's Early Apartments*, Cornell University Press, 1990.

Thomas Carter and Peter Goss, *Utah's Historic Architecture, 1847-1940*, Salt Lake City, Utah; University of Utah and Utah State Historical Society, 1988.

www.ingramcontent.com/pod-product-compliance
Lightning Source LLC
Chambersburg PA
CBHW041156290426
44108CB00003B/91